C000140173

Keto Juice

Easy Keto Juice Recipes to Lose Weight, Gain Enery, and Feel Great in Your Body

Jadahe Morris

© Copyright 2019 Jadahe Morris- All Rights Reserved.

In no way is it legal to reproduce, duplicate, or transmit any part of this document by either electronic means or in printed format. Recording of this publication is strictly prohibited, and any storage of this material is not allowed unless with written permission from the publisher. All rights reserved.

The information provided herein is stated to be truthful and consistent, in that any liability, regarding inattention or otherwise, by any usage or abuse of any policies, processes, or directions contained within is the solitary and complete responsibility of the recipient reader. Under no circumstances will any legal liability or blame be held against the publisher for any reparation, damages, or monetary loss due to the information herein, either directly or indirectly.

Respective authors own all copyrights not held by the publisher.

Legal Notice:

This book is copyright protected. This is only for personal use. You cannot amend, distribute, sell, use, quote or paraphrase any part of the content within this book without the consent of the author or copyright owner. Legal action will be pursued if this is breached.

Disclaimer Notice:

Please note the information contained within this document is for educational and entertainment purposes only. Every attempt has been made to provide accurate, up-to-date and reliable, complete information. No warranties of any kind are expressed or implied. Readers acknowledge that the author is not engaging in the rendering of legal, financial, medical or professional advice.

By reading this document, the reader agrees that under no circumstances are we responsible for any losses, direct or indirect, which are incurred as a result of the use of information contained within this document, including, but not limited to, errors, omissions, or inaccuracies.

Table of contents

Introduction

The ketogenic diet is the latest trend in the healthiest diets. The ketogenic diet is all about getting carbs and sugar out of the food. For this, Keto-ers turns to high-fat meats, nutritious vegetables, and fruits. So, no starchy vegetables like potatoes, no grains in any form, no bread, no crackers and no processed food.

One way to get started with the Ketogenic diet is to cook a proper high-fat and low-carb meal. And, Ketogenic cooking is effortless and easy. Another effective way to incorporate healthy veggies and fruits in your lifestyle is through juicing. It's the easiest to support your ketogenic diet goals. With the flavorful ingredients and meeting the macro requirements of keto food, you won't miss your regular juices at all.

Read on to know more about ketogenic lifestyle and how juicing complement this diet.

Chapter1: Understanding the Keto diet

The history of Keto

The ketogenic diet was actually invented for a medical purpose that was to treat epileptic patients, almost a century ago. Though there were already some remedies like fasting and other low-carb diets, physicians were looking for a more effective solution to control epilepsy. Hence, they discover a high-fat and low-carb diet which was name as Ketogenic diet. In the beginning, the Ketogenic diet was just a diet that switches the body into a fat burning machine completely, rather than the natural way to consuming carbs for energy. With time, Ketogenic turned out a successful and widely used treatment for epilepsy, especially for kids. And over the past 20 years, the interest of dieticians and health freaks in the Ketogenic diet is increased exponentially due to its amazing health benefits, and it is transformed as a lifestyle.

The process of ketosis

The meals of the Ketogenic diet contain 60 to 80 percent fats, 15 to 20 percent protein and 5 to 150 percent carbohydrates. Since this meal is low in carb; body ultimately goes into the state of ketosis. Ketosis is a natural process, in which small molecules "ketones' are used by the body cell as a fuel, instead of glucose. Ketones are the end product of fat burning procedure in the body when carbohydrate concentration gets too low. Usually, our body breakdown carbs into glucose for energy. And, in their absence or when the body runs out of carbs reserve and couldn't produce glucose, the body switches to fats, and as a result, fat burning hormones increase in blood. However, fat is a complex molecule and cannot be utilized directly. Therefore it is breakdown into ketones and then use as a fuel by the body cells, just like glucose.

In other words, when you eat fewer carbs and more fats, the body makes use of fats and produce fats to perform its vital activities.

Reaching ketosis

It is a little hard to reach ketosis as our body is not accustomed to functioning on fats regularly. The body takes time to adapt to burn fats. And, one cannot say precisely when the body is in ketosis or not because there are different degrees of ketosis.

The best and simple way to reach ketosis is to following Ketogenic diet to the T. And, this means consuming low carb and high-fat food as much as possible. You can make sure by making a note of your carb intake which should be not greater than 30 grams per day, and then limiting them gradually. If you want to achieve ketosis fast, you also need to pay attention to fats in your meals. A Ketogenic meal contains 70 to 80 percent fats of total calories. So, you must consume healthy fats in every meal such as fatty meats, avocado, nuts, avocado oil, and macadamia oil and coconut butter.

Once, your body enters into ketosis; you can maintain this state by doing a little exercise. When you exercise, body first uses carbs for energy, and when the carbs reserves are depleted, your body will turn to fats for energy to perform more physical activity. Start with a light exercise and then gradually increase its intensity; this will not only get your body into ketosis but will also speed it up – the best of both worlds.

Benefits of Ketogenic diet

The ketogenic diet is famous for its innumerable health benefits. Here are some benefits which you can get from the Ketogenic diet:

- Weight loss
- Improve digestion
- Control epileptic seizures

- Improve ache and sleep

- Decrease heartburns

- Enhanced memory

- Enhanced brain power

- Stabilize blood glucose, blood pressure, and cholesterol levels

- Treat tumor, cancer, Alzheimer and Parkinson disease

- Prevent metabolic and coronary diseases

Chapter2: Juicing Basics

How to make a juice

Natural juices are not only nutritious; they are also great to detox and cleanse your body. Store-bought juices are high in sugar and have preservatives and additives, and hence, they aren't a healthy choice at all. Even if the fruits are pasteurized, the nutrients are gone. Therefore, the most robust way to squeeze all the possible vitamins, nutrients and deliciousness out of your juicing ingredients is to make a juice at home.

To make juice at home, you just need to purchase a good juicer or blender. Next, you need to prepare your ingredients and for this, wash your juice ingredients and then cut them into small pieces. Switch on the juicer, then put the ingredients one at a time and process them to collect juices in the juicer's receptacle. You can either have the juice straightaway or pass the juice through a nut milk bag placed on top of a bowl and then have it.

Here are some more details to juice to the T at home.

- Buy Ingredients in Bulk

Fruits go expensive when they are not in season. So, if you want to get nutrients of any fruits, irrespective to the season, you need to buy them in bulk. Moreover, take advantage of the sale on juicing ingredients to save money as well. For example, a bag of avocado is ideal for Keto juices and smoothies and a perfect example to purchase in bulk and save money. You can then store the leftover fruit in freezer or refrigerator for later usage.

- Plan Your Juices

Certain fruits take time to be prepared for juicing; for example, they need peeling, coring etcetera. Therefore, you need to prepare your ingredients ahead. One way is to make batches of juicing ingredients for a week on Sunday and store them in Ziploc plastic bags or containers. It will take 30 to 45 minutes to get your ingredients washed up, cut and store. And, when you are ready to have your juice, just grab a batch of ingredients of your juice and run them through your juicer. A tip – to prevent your ingredients turning from browning, drizzle lemon juice over them once they are cut.

Tips for storing juice

A good practice of efficient juicing is juice once for a whole day. Yes, it's best to drink juice after being processed, but you can extend the life and freshness of juice to have it later in the day as a snack by storing it properly.

Here are some best tactics for juice storage without degrading their nutrient as much as possible and getting the most out of your juice:

- Story juice in wide mouth mason jars, about 8, 16 or 32-ounce filling space. You can also use amber jars, plastic bottles, stainless steel water bottle or thermos.

- Store juice as soon as you prepare it.

- Make sure you remove air from the storage container. First, fill the container with juice to the brim, pour in purified water if juice is enough. Then cover the container with a lid and seal tightly with either a vacuum sealing device or food saver appliance. Now, you can store juice for the long-term in the freezer.

- Mark the outside of storage container with the name and ingredients of juice and the date when the juice was processed.

- Store the juice containers in the refrigerator or freezer.

Another way to store juice is by freezing it in ice cube trays. If you have a large volume of juice, freeze it in plastic water bottles or milk-type jugs. And, defrost or thaw juice in the refrigerator and then consume it.

You can store juice in the refrigerator for 24 to 48 hours and up to 72 hours at the most. And, if you want to store the juice longer than that, then freeze it. If you are traveling, then use cooler bags with ice packs to store juice.

Produce Preparation Guide

Here are some tips to guide you through preparing your product for juicing.

1. Make sure your produce is as clean as possible and therefore, rinse and wash produce thoroughly by using a produce or antimicrobial wash.

2. For peeling your produce, you must know if it affects your juice flavor or not. If peel doesn't effect the flavor of juice, leave the skin on. Moreover, the outer layer of many produce has beneficial nutrients.

3. Seeds and pits can sometimes lend a bitter flavor in juice and can damage blades, so it's better to remove them.

4. For nuts, remove shells if necessary or else keep the skin on, for example, the skin of almonds contain lots a flavor and add texture to juice, so don't remove their shell.

5. Clean the bottoms of produce thoroughly, for example, beets. Also, remove their top ends like carrots.

6. Don't cut off stem from leafy vegetables; they contain lots of flavor and juice. But do wash them through as they usually have most dirt.

7. Cut large produce in small pieces, preferably quarters, to process at consistent rate.

How to Pick the Right Juicer

There are two most common types of home juicer:

Centrifugal Juicer: One type is centrifugal juicer that is an excellent choice for juicing fruits and most of the veggies, except for greens and wheatgrass. Furthermore, a centrifugal juicer is a speedy machine so they can prepare a fresh glass of juice for you quickly each morning. So, if you are mostly short of time, centrifugal juicer may be right for you. Another benefit of the centrifugal juicer is their affordable price which starts from $20 and may increase to $200 for its higher-end models. So, if centrifugal juicer suits you best, then purchase the one which is easy to clean as well. Look for those model that easily snaps apart and wash with minimal efforts. In comparison to all these great benefits, centrifugal juicer has one flaw – they are noisier. The noise produced is on par with a typical food processor, blender or coffee blender.

Masticating Juicer: Another type of juicer is high-end masticating juicer that is also sometimes called slow juicer or cold press. It is perfect for health freaks because this juicer produces the most healthful and nutrient dense juice, especially of leafy greens. Yes, they are slow, but their low rpm helps in extracting the most juice from greens. Another huge perk of the low processing speed of this juicer is that very little heat is introduced into the juice and therefore, juice can be stored for up to 48 hours, without deteriorating its nutrition. The only drawback of the masticating juicer is their high price which runs upward of $200. But every dollar is worth investing in this juicer for your health, and you will recuperate your money over time.

Health Benefits of Juicing

Juicing, when done right, is beneficial for improving your health, such as:

- A fun way to add more vegetables and fruits to diet,
- Get more nutrition to the body,
- An excellent way to consume a variety of veggies and fruits,
- Helps fighting cancer,

- Lowers high cholesterol,

- Detoxify the body,

- Reduces blood sugar levels,

- Help in getting better skin,

- Escalate weight loss,

- Boost the immune system,

- Increase mental alertness,

- Increase energy level,

- Helps with longevity and leading a better life.

Chapter3: FAQ

Question 1: Is juicing only for health nuts?

Answer: Juicing used to be a healthy food for people who held extreme views about foods and supplements but today, things are different. People have become more aware of leading a fit life and are looking for healthy diets that promote organic, whole and unprocessed food, and in all this, juices have become an essential part. People belonging to every walk of life are happy to consume juices in regards to doing something healthy for their body.

Question 2: What will I fell if I start juicing regularly?

Answer: It is recommended to take juicing slowly at first, and once the body is used to it, you can adopt it as a healthy diet regularly. Your digestive system will respond immediately to this change in diet, and within two weeks, you will feel more energetic. Your skin will glow, hairs and nails will get healthier. Last but not least, juicing will speed up weight loss.

Question 3: How much will it cost me to get started with juicing?

Answer: If you have a juicer, then juicing will not cost you a dime, except for veggies and fruits expenditure. A great way to save money on juicing is to purchase produce in bulk.

And, with the desire to eat more fresh fruits and vegetables, you will save money because you be buying meat, junk or processed food in less quantity.

If you don't have a juicer, you will need to do an expenditure of around $100 to $500, based on the juicer that suits your needs. This spending is a better investment in your healthy future.

Chapter4: Fruit Based Juices and Smoothies

Raspberry Lemon Juice

Servings: 1

Preparation time: 5 minutes

Nutrition Value:

Calories: 289 Cal, Carbs: 14 g, Fat: 85 g, Protein: 1 g, Fiber: 6.5 g.

Ingredients:

- ½ lemon, seeded

- ½ lime, seeded

- ½ cup fresh raspberries

- ½ tablespoon erythritol sweetener

- 2 tablespoons avocado oil

- 1 cup filtered water, chilled

- Mint for garnishing

Method:

1. Place berries into ice cube tray, fill with water and freeze for 2 hours.

2. Then juice lime and lemon and pour into a serving glass.

3. Pour in water, add sweetener and oil and mix well until combined.

4. Add frozen raspberry ice cubes, garnish with mint and serve.

Grapefruit Ginger Juice

Servings: 2

Preparation time: 5 minutes

Nutrition Value:

Calories: 359 Cal, Carbs: 26 g, Fat: 27.1 g, Protein: 1.8 g, Fiber: 5.1 g.

Ingredients:

- 1-inch piece of ginger, peeled

- 3 cups baby spinach leaves, packed

- 2 medium grapefruits, peel and pith removed

- 4 tablespoons avocado oil

Method:

1. Place juicer collector under the nozzle of juicer, switch it on and process ginger, spinach, and grapefruits until thoroughly juiced.

2. Then add oil and stir well.

3. Pour juice into chilled glasses and serve straightaway.

Kiwi Juice

Servings: 1

Preparation time: 5 minutes

Nutrition Value:

Calories: 385 Cal, Carbs: 33.6 g, Fat: 27.4 g, Protein: 0.9 g, Fiber: 19.1 g.

Ingredients:

- 3 handfuls of baby spinach

- 2 kiwis, peeled

- 1 green apple, cored

- 1/8 teaspoon sea salt

- 1 lime, rind removed

- 2 tablespoons avocado oil

- 1/2 cup filtered water, chilled

Method:

1. Prepare vegetables and fruits and rinse them thoroughly.

2. Place juicer collector under the nozzle of juicer, switch it on and process all the

   ingredients until thoroughly juiced.

3. Add salt and oil into prepared juice, stir well and then pour in water.

4. Pour juice into a chilled glass and serve straightaway.

Raspberry Lemonade Smoothies

Servings: 4

Preparation time: 5 minutes

Nutrition Value:

Calories: 287 Cal, Carbs: 7.5 g, Fat: 23.5 g, Protein: 11.4 g, Fiber: 4.2 g.

Ingredients:

- 1 cup frozen raspberries

- 1/4 cup powdered Swerve Sweetener

- 1 teaspoon lemon zest

- 1/3 cup fresh lemon juice

- 2 tablespoons avocado oil

- 2 ounces cream cheese

- 1 cup yogurt

- 1/3 cup filtered water, chilled

- 2 cups ice

Method:

1. Place all the ingredients in a blender and pulse at high speed for 1 to 2 minutes or until smooth.

2. Divide smoothie evenly between 4 glasses and serve.

Strawberry Crunch Smoothie

Servings: 1

Preparation time: 5 minutes

Nutrition Value:

Calories: 324 Cal, Carbs: 14.6 g, Fat: 26.6 g, Protein: 6.5 g, Fiber: 7 g.

Ingredients:

- ½ cup frozen strawberries
- ½ teaspoon cinnamon
- 2 tablespoon almonds
- 1 tablespoon chia seeds
- 1 tablespoon avocado oil
- 1 cup almond milk, unsweetened and full-fat

Method:

1. Place all the ingredients in a blender and pulse at high speed for 1 to 2 minutes or until smooth.
2. Pour smoothie into serving glass.

Blueberry Smoothie

Servings: 1

Preparation time: 5 minutes

Nutrition Value:

Calories: 659 Cal, Carbs: 3 g, Fat: 27 g, Protein: 31 g, Fiber: 1.2 g.

Ingredients:

- ¼ cup blueberries

- 1 scoop whey protein powder

- 1 teaspoon vanilla essence, unsweetened

- 1 teaspoon avocado oil

- 1 cup coconut milk, unsweetened and full-fat

Method:

1. Place all the ingredients in a blender and pulse at high speed for 1 to 2 minutes or until smooth.

2. Pour smoothie into serving glass.

Blueberry Coconut Chia Smoothie

Servings: 1

Preparation time: 5 minutes

Nutrition Value:

Calories: 237.3 Cal, Carbs: 5.7 g, Fat: 21.07 g, Protein: 6.23 g, Fiber: 3.5 g.

Ingredients:

- 1 cup frozen blueberries

- 2 tablespoons ground chia seed

- 2 tablespoons swerve sweetener

- 2 tablespoons avocado oil

- 1 cup coconut milk yogurt

- 1/2 cup coconut cream

- 1 cup unsweetened almond milk, unsweetened and full-fat

Method:

1. Place all the ingredients in a blender and pulse at high speed for 1 to 2 minutes or until smooth.

2. Pour smoothie evening between four glasses and serve.

Strawberry Protein Smoothie

Servings: 1

Preparation time: 5 minutes

Nutrition Value:

Calories: 304 Cal, Carbs: 10.6 g, Fat: 23.3 g, Protein: 13 g, Fiber: 3.4 g.

Ingredients:

- 1/3 cup frozen strawberries

- ½ scoop protein whey powder

- 1 tablespoon almond butter

- 1 tablespoon avocado oil

- 1/3 cup filtered water, chilled

- ½ cup almond milk, unsweetened and full-fat

Method:

1. Place all the ingredients in a blender and pulse at high speed for 1 to 2 minutes or until smooth.

2. Pour smoothie into a glass and serve.

Milkshake Smoothie with Raspberries

Servings: 2

Preparation time: 5 minutes

Nutrition Value:

Calories: 157 Cal, Carbs: 3.5 g, Fat: 15 g, Protein: 2 g, Fiber: 1.5 g.

Ingredients:

- 1/4 cup fresh raspberries

- 1/8 teaspoon salt

- 2 tablespoons swerve sweetener

- 1/2 teaspoon vanilla extract, unsweetened

- 1 tablespoon avocado oil

- 1 tablespoon cream cheese

- 1/4 cup heavy whipping cream

- 1 cup almond milk, unsweetened and full-fat

- 4 ounces crushed ice

Method:

1. Place cream cheese in a heatproof bowl and microwave for 5 seconds or until soft.

2. Add to blender along with remaining ingredients and pulse at high speed for 1 to 2 minutes or until smooth.

3. Pour smoothie between 2 glasses and serve.

Vanilla Blackberry Lemonade

Servings: 1

Preparation time: 5 minutes

Nutrition Value:

Calories: 202 Cal, Carbs: 17 g, Fat: 69 g, Protein: 14 g, Fiber: 5.8 g.

Ingredients:

- 1/2 cup fresh blackberries

- ½ teaspoon glucomannan

- 2 pinches salt

- ½ teaspoon stevia extract

- 1 tablespoon collagen

- 1 teaspoon vanilla extract, unsweetened

- 1/4 cup lemon juice

- 1 tablespoon avocado oil

- 2/3 cup almond milk, unsweetened and full-fat

- 3 cups ice cubes

Method:

1. Place all the ingredients in a blender, except for berries, glucomannan and ice cubes.

2. Pulse at low speed until just mixed, then blend in glucomannan and switch on the blender.

3. Add berries and ice and continue blending at high speed until smooth.

4. Pour smoothie into a glass and serve.

Coconut Milk Strawberry Smoothie

Servings: 2

Preparation time: 5 minutes

Nutrition Value:

Calories: 397 Cal, Carbs: 14.4 g, Fat: 80 g, Protein: 5.7 g, Fiber: 5 g.

Ingredients:

- 1 cup frozen strawberries
- 2 tablespoons stevia
- 2 tablespoons almond butter
- 1 tablespoon avocado oil
- 1 cup coconut milk, unsweetened and full-fat

Method:

1. Place all the ingredients in a blender and pulse at high speed for 1 to 2 minutes or until smooth.
2. Pour smoothie into a glass and serve.

Strawberry Cheesecake Smoothie

Servings: 1

Preparation time: 5 minutes

Nutrition Value:

Calories: 370 Cal, Carbs: 12.5 g, Fat: 24 g, Protein: 17.5 g, Fiber: 2.5 g.

Ingredients:

- 1/2 cup strawberries, fresh
- 4 tablespoons swerve sweetener
- 1/2 teaspoon vanilla extract, unsweetened
- 1/2 cup cottage cheese
- 2 ounces cream cheese
- 1/4 cup almond milk, unsweetened
- 1 cup ice cubes

Method:

1. Place all the ingredients in a blender and pulse at high speed for 1 to 2 minutes or until smooth.

2. Pour smoothie into a glass and serve.

Red Velvet Smoothie

Servings: 2

Preparation time: 5 minutes

Nutrition Value:

Calories: 341 Cal, Carbs: 13.6 g, Fat: 30 g, Protein: 4.3 g, Fiber: 6.1 g.

Ingredients:

- 1/2 of a medium avocado

- 1/2 small beetroot

- 2 tablespoons erythritol sweetener

- 3 tablespoons cacao powder, unsweetened

- 3 tablespoons avocado oil

- 1/4 teaspoon vanilla extract, unsweetened

- 2 cups coconut milk, unsweetened

- 2 cups ice cubes

Method:

1. Place all the ingredients in a blender and pulse at high speed for 1 to 2 minutes or until smooth.

2. Pour smoothie into a glass and serve.

Tropical Smoothie

Servings: 1

Preparation time: 5 minutes

Nutrition Value:

Calories: 340.6 Cal, Carbs: 7.4 g, Fat: 32.6 g, Protein: 4.4 g, Fiber: 3 g.

Ingredients:

- 2 tablespoons flaxseed meal

- 20 drops liquid Stevia

- ½ teaspoon mango extract, unsweetened

- ¼ teaspoon blueberry extract, unsweetened

- ¼ teaspoon banana extract, unsweetened

- 1 tablespoon avocado oil

- ¼ cup sour cream

- ¾ cup coconut milk, unsweetened and full-fat

- 7 large ice cubes

Method:

1. Place all the ingredients in a blender and let rest for 5 minutes or until flaxseed meal soak some of the moisture.

2. Then pulse at high speed for 1 to 2 minutes or until smooth.

3. Pour smoothie into a glass and serve.

Avocado Smoothie

Servings: 2

Preparation time: 5 minutes

Nutrition Value:

Calories: 208 Cal, Carbs: 5 g, Fat: 21 g, Protein: 1 g, Fiber: 1 g.

Ingredients:

- 1/2 of a medium avocado

- ½ inch piece of ginger

- 1/2 teaspoon turmeric

- 1 tablespoon erythritol sweetener

- 1 teaspoon lemon juice

- 3/4 cup coconut milk, unsweetened and full-fat

- 1/4 cup almond milk, unsweetened and full-fat

- 1 cup crushed ice

Method:

1. Place all the ingredients in a blender, except for sweetener and ice.

2. Then pulse at high speed for 1 to 2 minutes or until smooth.

3. Pour smoothie into two glasses and serve.

Strawberry Avocado Smoothie

Servings: 5

Preparation time: 5 minutes

Nutrition Value:

Calories: 208 Cal, Carbs: 9.8 g, Fat: 18.3 g, Protein: 1 g, Fiber: 3.7 g.

Ingredients:

- 1-pound frozen strawberries

- 1 large avocado

- 1/4 cup erythritol sweetener

- 5 tablespoons avocado oil

- 1 1/2 cup almond milk, unsweetened and full-fat

Method:

1. Place all the ingredients in a blender and pulse at high speed for 1 to 2 minutes or until smooth.

2. Pour smoothie into two glasses and serve.

Blueberry Ginger Smoothie

Servings: 2

Preparation time: 5 minutes

Nutrition Value:

Calories: 189 Cal, Carbs: 5 g, Fat: 17 g, Protein: 4 g, Fiber: 1 g.

Ingredients:

- 2 slices of apple

- 15 blueberries

- 3 slices of ginger

- 1 tablespoon erythritol sweetener

- 1/2 tablespoon collagen powder

- 1 teaspoon avocado oil

- 1/2 cup coconut yogurt

- 1 cup coconut milk, unsweetened and full-fat

Method:

1. Place all the ingredients in a blender and pulse at high speed for 1 to 2 minutes or until smooth.

2. Pour smoothie into two glasses and serve.

Peach Pie Protein Shake

Servings: 1

Preparation time: 5 minutes

Nutrition Value:

Calories: 421 Cal, Carbs: 20 g, Fat: 31.8 g, Protein: 14.7 g, Fiber: 3.3 g.

Ingredients:

- 1 peach, pitted

- 1 scoop vanilla protein powder

- 1/8 teaspoon cinnamon

- 2 tablespoons avocado oil

- 1/4 cup yogurt

- 2/3 cup almond milk

- 10 cubes of ice

Method:

1. Place all the ingredients in a blender and pulse at high speed for 1 to 2 minutes or until smooth.

2. Pour smoothie into two glasses and serve.

Chapter5: Vegetables-Based Juices & Smoothies

Beets Breakfast Juice

Servings: 5

Preparation time: 5 minutes

Nutrition Value:

Calories: 659 Cal, Carbs: 9.7 g, Fat: 55.5 g, Protein: 30.9 g, Fiber: 2.8 g.

Ingredients:

- 1 carrot, top removed

- 2 beets, peeled and top removed

- 2 apples, seeded and cored

- 2 lemons, peeled

- 2 tablespoons avocado oil

Method:

1. Prepare vegetables and fruits and rinse them thoroughly.

2. Then cut carrot and beets into long slices and cut apples into small pieces.

3. Place juicer collector under the nozzle of juicer, switch it on and process all the ingredients until thoroughly juiced.

4. Add avocado oil into prepared juice, stir well and pour into chilled glasses.

5. Serve straightaway.

Celery Kale Juice

Servings: 1

Preparation time: 5 minutes

Nutrition Value:

Calories: 300 Cal, Carbs: 14 g, Fat: 82 g, Protein: 4 g, Fiber: 6.4 g.

Ingredients:

- 4 kale leaves

- 1 cup spinach leaves

- 3 medium stalks of celery

- 1 medium cucumber, peeled

- 1-inch piece of ginger, peeled

- 1 lemon, peeled, halved and seeded

- 2 tablespoons avocado oil

Method:

1. Prepare vegetables and rinse them thoroughly.

2. Then cut celery, cucumber, and ginger into quarters.

3. Place juicer collector under the nozzle of juicer, switch it on and process all the ingredients until thoroughly juiced.

4. Add oil into prepared juice and stir well.

5. Pour juice into a chilled glass and serve straightaway.

Zucchini Juice

Servings: 1

Preparation time: 5 minutes

Nutrition Value:

Calories: 466 Cal, Carbs: 34.9 g, Fat: 34.17 g, Protein: 4.66 g, Fiber: 27 g.

Ingredients:

- 1 large zucchini

- 1 green apple, cored

- 1 medium cucumber, peeled

- 1-inch piece of ginger, peeled

- 1 lemon, peeled and seeded

- 2 tablespoons avocado oil

Method:

1. Prepare vegetables and fruits and rinse them thoroughly.

2. Then cut apple, cucumber, and ginger into quarters.

3. Place juicer collector under the nozzle of juicer, switch it on and process all the

   ingredients until thoroughly juiced.

4. Add oil into the juice and stir well.

5. Pour juice into a chilled serving glass and serve straightaway.

Radish Juice

Servings: 1

Preparation time: 5 minutes

Nutrition Value:

Calories: 690 Cal, Carbs: 44.85 g, Fat: 55.2 g, Protein: 3.45 g, Fiber: 29.2 g.

Ingredients:

- 1 bunch of radishes

- 2 medium green apples, peeled and cored

- 2 stalks of celery

- 1 large beet, peeled

- 2 tablespoons avocado oil

Method:

1. Prepare vegetables and fruits and rinse them thoroughly.

2. Then cut radish, apple, and beets into quarters.

3. Place juicer collector under the nozzle of juicer, switch it on and process all the ingredients until thoroughly juiced.

4. Add oil into the juice and stir well.

5. Pour juice into a chilled serving glass and serve straightaway.

Celery Juice

Servings: 1

Preparation time: 5 minutes

Nutrition Value:

Calories: 401 Cal, Carbs: 34 g, Fat: 28.1 g, Protein: 3 g, Fiber: 27.3 g.

Ingredients:

- 1 large green apple, seeded

- 1 small bunch of celery

- 1/2 of a medium cucumber, peeled

- 1 -inch knob of ginger, peeled

- 1/2 of lemon, seeded

- 2 tablespoons avocado oil

Method:

1. Prepare vegetables and fruits and rinse them thoroughly.

2. Then cut apple, celery, and cucumber into quarters.

3. Place juicer collector under the nozzle of juicer, switch it on and process all the

   ingredients until thoroughly juiced.

4. Add oil into prepared juice and stir well.

5. Pour juice into a chilled glass and serve straightaway.

Spinach Juice

Servings: 2

Preparation time: 5 minutes

Nutrition Value:

Calories: 298.5 Cal, Carbs: 11.9 g, Fat: 27.2 g, Protein: 1.5 g, Fiber: 7.3 g.

Ingredients:

- 2 cups chopped spinach

- 1 medium apple, cored and chopped

- 1 stalk of celery

- 1/2 of lime, peeled and seeded

- 4 tablespoons avocado oil

- 3/4 cup filtered water, chilled

Method:

1. Prepare vegetables and fruits and rinse them thoroughly.

2. Then cut apple and celery into quarters.

3. Place juicer collector under the nozzle of juicer, switch it on and process all the

   ingredients until thoroughly juiced.

4. Add oil into the prepared juice, pour in water and stir well.

5. Pour juice into chilled glasses and serve straightaway.

Celery and Spinach Juice

Servings: 1

Preparation time: 5 minutes

Nutrition Value:

Calories: 335 Cal, Carbs: 20.1 g, Fat: 27.5 g, Protein: 1.6 g, Fiber: 6.8 g.

Ingredients:

- ½ of green apple, seeded

- 1 medium cucumber, peeled

- 2 handful spinach

- 3 medium stalks of celery

- ½ of a lemon, seeded

- 2 tablespoons avocado oil

Method:

1. Prepare vegetables and rinse them thoroughly.

2. Then cut apple and apple into quarters.

3. Place juicer collector under the nozzle of juicer, switch it on and process all the

   ingredients until thoroughly juiced.

4. Add oil into the prepared juice and stir well.

5. Pour juice into a chilled glass and serve straightaway.

Swiss Chard Juice

Servings: 1

Preparation time: 5 minutes

Nutrition Value:

Calories: 353 Cal, Carbs: 21.2 g, Fat: 27.8 g, Protein: 4.4 g, Fiber: 9.1 g.

Ingredients:

- 4 large Swiss chard leaves

- 1 bunch celery

- 1 medium cucumber, peeled

- ½ bunch of cilantro

- 1-inch piece of ginger, peeled

- 1 lemon, peeled

- 1 lime, peeled

- 2 tablespoons avocado oil

Method:

1. Prepare vegetables by chopping them all and then rinse well.

2. Place juicer collector under the nozzle of juicer, switch it on and process all the ingredients until thoroughly juiced.

3. Add oil into prepared juice and stir well.

4. Pour juice into a chilled glass and serve straightaway.

Tomato Juice

Servings: 1

Preparation time: 5 minutes

Nutrition Value:

Calories: 351 Cal, Carbs: 22 g, Fat: 27.6 g, Protein: 3.5 g, Fiber: 15.3 g.

Ingredients:

- 2 large tomatoes, cored

- 1 medium stalk of celery

- 1 medium cucumber, peeled

- ¼ cup parsley

- ½ teaspoon sea salt

- 1/8 teaspoon cayenne pepper

- 2 tablespoons avocado oil

- ½ cup crushed ice

Method:

1. Prepare vegetables and rinse them thoroughly.

2. Then cut cucumber and tomatoes into quarters.

3. Place juicer collector under the nozzle of juicer, switch it on and process all the ingredients until thoroughly juiced.

4. Add oil and ice into prepared juice and stir well.

5. Pour juice into a chilled glass and serve straightaway.

Cauliflower Juice

Servings: 2

Preparation time: 5 minutes

Nutrition Value:

Calories: 525 Cal, Carbs: 48.5 g, Fat: 34.4 g, Protein: 5.2 g, Fiber: 34.2 g.

Ingredients:

- 1 medium head of cauliflower, cut into small florets

- ½ bunch of spinach leaves

- 1 medium green apple, peeled and seeded

- 1 pomegranate, seeds only

- 1-inch piece of ginger

- 4 tablespoons avocado oil

Method:

1. Prepare vegetables and fruits and rinse them thoroughly.

2. Then cut cauliflower into small florets and apple into quarters.

3. Place juicer collector under the nozzle of juicer, switch it on and process all the

   ingredients until thoroughly juiced.

4. Add oil into prepared juice and stir well.

5. Pour juice into a chilled glass and serve straightaway.

Celery and Parsley Juice

Servings: 1

Preparation time: 5 minutes

Nutrition Value:

Calories: 307 Cal, Carbs: 12.3 g, Fat: 27.3 g, Protein: 3 g, Fiber: 6 g.

Ingredients:

- 2 medium stalks of celery

- 3 leaves of Swiss chard

- ½ inch turmeric, peeled

- 1 handful of parsley

- 1 lime, peeled and seeded

- 2 tablespoons avocado oil

Method:

1. Prepare vegetables and rinse them thoroughly.

2. Place juicer collector under the nozzle of juicer, switch it on and process all the ingredients except for lemon and water, until thoroughly juiced.

3. Add oil into prepared juice and stir well.

4. Pour juice into a chilled glass and serve straightaway.

Cucumber and Mint Juice

Servings: 1

Preparation time: 5 minutes

Nutrition Value:

Calories: 298 Cal, Carbs: 10.43 g, Fat: 27.5 g, Protein: 2.2 g, Fiber: 5.1 g.

Ingredients:

- 4 medium stalks of celery

- ½ of a medium cucumber, peeled

- 1 handful of parsley

- 1 handful of mint

- ½ of a medium lemon, peeled

- 2 tablespoons avocado oil

Method:

1. Prepare vegetables and fruits and rinse them thoroughly.

2. Then cut the cucumber into quarters.

3. Place juicer collector under the nozzle of juicer, switch it on and process all the ingredients until thoroughly juiced.

4. Add oil into prepared juice and stir well.

5. Pour juice into a chilled glass and serve straightaway.

Bell Pepper Juice

Servings: 1

Preparation time: 5 minutes

Nutrition Value:

Calories: 334 Cal, Carbs: 16.7 g, Fat: 27.8 g, Protein: 4.2 g, Fiber: 7.7 g.

Ingredients:

- 1 medium cucumber, peeled

- 1 medium red bell pepper, cored

- ¼ of a medium head of romaine lettuce

- 1 handful of parsley

- 2 tablespoons avocado oil

Method:

1. Prepare vegetables and rinse them thoroughly.

2. Place juicer collector under the nozzle of juicer, switch it on and process all the ingredients until thoroughly juiced.

3. Add oil into prepared juice and stir well.

4. Pour juice into a chilled glass and serve straightaway.

Kale Juice

Servings: 1

Preparation time: 5 minutes

Nutrition Value:

Calories: 300 Cal, Carbs: 10.5 g, Fat: 27.3 g, Protein: 3 g, Fiber: 4.7 g.

Ingredients:

- 3 leaves of kale, chopped

- 3 handful of spinach

- 4 medium stalks of celery

- 1 medium cucumber, peeled

- 2 tablespoons avocado oil

Method:

1. Prepare vegetables and rinse them thoroughly.

2. Place juicer collector under the nozzle of juicer, switch it on and process all the

   ingredients until thoroughly juiced.

3. Add oil into prepared juice and stir well.

4. Pour juice into a chilled glass and serve straightaway.

Parsley Smoothie

Servings: 1

Preparation time: 5 minutes

Nutrition Value:

Calories: 350 Cal, Carbs: 21.8 g, Fat: 27.6 g, Protein: 3.5 g, Fiber: 8.4 g.

Ingredients:

- 1 orange, seeded and peeled

- 1 medium cucumber, peeled

- 1-inch piece of ginger

- ¼ cup spinach

- ¼ cup parsley

- 1 lemon, seeded and peeled

- 2 tablespoons avocado oil

- 1 cup filtered water

- 1 cup ice cubes

Method:

1. Prepare vegetables and rinse them thoroughly.

2. Cur orange, cucumber, ginger and lemon into small pieces and add to a blender.

3. Add remaining ingredients and pulse at high speed for 1 to 2 minutes or until

    smooth.

4. Pour smoothie into a glass, then stir in oil until mixed and serve.

Winter Green Juice

Servings: 1

Preparation time: 5 minutes

Nutrition Value:

Calories: 679 Cal, Carbs: 40.7 g, Fat: 55 g, Protein: 5.1 g, Fiber: 31.1 g.

Ingredients:

- 1 medium green apple, peeled and cored

- ½ of a medium cucumber

- 1/4 of a medium head of green cabbage

- 6 leaves of romaine lettuce

- 4 sprigs of fresh mint

- 1-inch piece of ginger

- 2 tablespoons avocado oil

Method:

1. Prepare vegetables and fruits and rinse them thoroughly.

2. Then cut apple and cucumber into quarters and slice cabbage into wedges.

3. Place juicer collector under the nozzle of juicer, switch it on and process all the ingredients until thoroughly juiced.

4. Add oil into prepared juice and stir well.

5. Pour juice into a chilled glass and serve straightaway.

Cucumber Smoothie

Servings: 2

Preparation time: 5 minutes

Nutrition Value:

Calories: 299 Cal, Carbs: 4.5 g, Fat: 30.9 g, Protein: 0.7 g, Fiber: 3.7 g.

Ingredients:

- 1 large cucumber, peeled and sliced

- 2 ounces avocado, peeled and sliced

- 2 teaspoons Green Tea powder

- 1/2 teaspoon lemon liquid stevia

- 1 teaspoon lemon juice

- 4 tablespoons avocado oil

- 8 ounces of water

- 1/2 cup ice cubes

Method:

1. Place all the ingredients in a blender and pulse at high speed for 1 to 2 minutes or until smooth.

2. Divide smoothie evenly between two glasses and serve.

Mint Coco Smoothie

Servings: 1

Preparation time: 5 minutes

Nutrition Value:

Calories: 531 Cal, Carbs: 19.9 g, Fat: 39.5 g, Protein: 23.4 g, Fiber: 10.6 g.

Ingredients:

- 1/2 cup frozen cauliflower florets

- 1/2 sliced avocado

- 1 tablespoon chopped mint

- 1 tablespoon cacao powder, unsweetened

- 1 scoop collagen protein

- 1 teaspoon vanilla extract, unsweetened

- 1.5 tablespoon avocado oil

- 4-ounce coconut milk, full-fat and unsweetened

- 4-ounce filtered water

Method:

1. Place all the ingredients in a blender and pulse at high speed for 1 to 2 minutes or until smooth.

2. Pour smoothie into a glass and serve.

Chapter6: Green Juices and Smoothies

Green Breakfast Smoothie

Servings: 1

Preparation time: 5 minutes

Nutrition Value:

Calories: 387 Cal, Carbs: 12.5 g, Fat: 27.1 g, Protein: 23.2 g, Fiber: 6.8 g.

Ingredients:

- 1-ounce spinach leaves

- 2-ounce sliced cucumber

- 2-ounce sliced celery

- 2-ounce sliced avocado

- 1 scoop whey protein powder

- 10 drops liquid stevia

- 1 tablespoon avocado oil

- 1 1/2 cups almond milk, unsweetened and full-fat

- 1/2 teaspoon chia seeds, for garnishing

Method:

1. Prepare all the ingredients and place in a blender, except for chia seeds.

2. Pulse at high speed for 1 to 2 minutes or until smooth.

3. Pour smoothie into a glass and serve.

Green Protein Smoothie

Servings: 1

Preparation time: 5 minutes

Nutrition Value:

Calories: 346 Cal, Carbs: 9 g, Fat: 25.4 g, Protein: 21.6 g, Fiber: 5.8 g.

Ingredients:

- 1/2 of a medium avocado, sliced

- 1 cup spinach leaves, chopped

- 1 scoop of whey protein powder

- 10 drops of stevia

- 1/4 teaspoon peppermint extract

- 1 tablespoon avocado oil

- 1/2 cup almond milk, unsweetened and full-fat

- 1 cup ice cubes

Method:

1. Prepare all the ingredients and place in a blender.

2. Pulse at high speed for 1 to 2 minutes or until smooth.

3. Pour smoothie into a glass and serve.

Mint Coco Green Smoothie

Servings: 1

Preparation time: 5 minutes

Nutrition Value:

Calories: 380 Cal, Carbs: 13.3 g, Fat: 27 g, Protein: 20.9 g, Fiber: 7 g.

Ingredients:

- 1/2 cup frozen cauliflower florets

- ½ of a medium avocado

- 1 tablespoon chopped mint

- 1/8 teaspoon sea salt

- 1 tablespoon cacao powder, unsweetened

- 1/8 teaspoon cinnamon

- 1 scoop of whey protein powder

- 1 teaspoon vanilla extract, unsweetened

- 1 tablespoon avocado oil

- 4-ounce coconut milk, unsweetened and full-fat

- 4-ounce filtered water

Method:

1. Prepare all the ingredients and place in a blender.

2. Pulse at high speed for 1 to 2 minutes or until smooth.

3. Pour smoothie into a glass and serve.

Chocolate Green Smoothie

Servings: 1

Preparation time: 5 minutes

Nutrition Value:

Calories: 848 Cal, Carbs: 25.4 g, Fat: 78 g, Protein: 10.6 g, Fiber: 11.5 g.

Ingredients:

- 2-ounce frozen raspberries

- 4 ounce chopped spinach

- 1 tablespoon swerve sweetener

- 1 tablespoon cocoa powder, unsweetened

- 1 cup coconut cream

Method:

1. Prepare all the ingredients and place in a blender.

2. Pulse at high speed for 1 to 2 minutes or until smooth.

3. Pour smoothie into a glass and serve.

Green Lemon Smoothie

Servings: 1

Preparation time: 5 minutes

Nutrition Value:

Calories: 339 Cal, Carbs: 12.7 g, Fat: 22.6 g, Protein: 21.5 g, Fiber: 2.2 g.

Ingredients:

- 1/2 of a large avocado, sliced

- 2 cups spinach leaves

- 1/2 of cucumber, sliced

- 1 scoop collagen protein powder

- 1 scoop whey protein powder

- 10 drops of stevia

- 3 tablespoons lemon juice

- 1 tablespoon avocado oil

- 1/2 cup coconut milk, unsweetened and full-fat

- 1 cup ice cubes

Method:

1. Prepare all the ingredients and place in a blender, except for collagen protein powder.

2. Pulse at high speed for 1 to 2 minutes or until smooth.

3. Then add collagen and blend on low speed until mixed.

4. Pour smoothie into a glass and serve.

Collagen Green Juice

Servings: 2

Preparation time: 5 minutes

Nutrition Value:

Calories: 204.5 Cal, Carbs: 10.7 g, Fat: 14 g, Protein: 8.7 g, Fiber: 2.2 g.

Ingredients:

- 2 medium cucumbers, chopped

- 1/2 bunch of celery, chopped

- 1 cup chopped parsley

- 1 cup chopped mint leaves

- 3 lemons, peeled and chopped

- 2 tablespoons avocado oil

- 1 scoop collagen powder

Method:

1. Prepare vegetables and rinse them thoroughly.

2. Place juicer collector under the nozzle of juicer, switch it on and process all the

   ingredients except for collagen until thoroughly juiced.

3. Add collagen into prepared juice, stir well until mixed and then stir in oil.

4. Divide juice between two chilled glasses and serve.

Green Ginger Juice

Servings: 1

Preparation time: 5 minutes

Nutrition Value:

Calories: 444 Cal, Carbs: 24 g, Fat: 64 g, Protein: 12 g, Fiber: 13.2 g.

Ingredients:

- 1 medium pear, sliced

- 6 leaves of romaine lettuce

- 2 celery roots

- 2 sprigs of rosemary

- 1-inch piece of ginger

- 1 scoop whey protein powder

- 1 tablespoon avocado oil

Method:

1. Prepare vegetables and rinse them thoroughly.

2. Place juicer collector under the nozzle of juicer, switch it on and process all the

   ingredients until thoroughly juiced.

3. Add oil and protein powder into prepared juice and stir well.

4. Pour juice into a chilled glass and serve straightaway.

Keto Flu Green Smoothie

Servings: 1

Preparation time: 5 minutes

Nutrition Value:

Calories: 144 Cal, Carbs: 11.5 g, Fat: 9.76 g, Protein: 2.5 g, Fiber: 5.7 g.

Ingredients:

- 2-ounce avocado, pitted and sliced

- 1/2 cup cucumber, peeled and sliced

- ½ cup kale

- 2 strawberries

- 1/2 teaspoon sea salt

- 1 teaspoon stevia

- 1 teaspoon vanilla extract, unsweetened

- 1/2 cup almond milk, unsweetened and full-fat

Method:

1. Prepare all the ingredients and place in a blender.

2. Pulse at high speed for 1 to 2 minutes or until smooth.

3. Pour smoothie into a glass and serve.

Citrus Green Smoothie

Servings: 1

Preparation time: 5 minutes

Nutrition Value:

Calories: 432 Cal, Carbs: 17.3 g, Fat: 31.2 g, Protein: 20.5 g, Fiber: 11.4 g.

Ingredients:

- ¼ cup spinach leaves

- 1 teaspoon orange zest

- 1 scoop whey protein powder

- 1/8 teaspoon xanthan gum

- 2 tablespoons avocado oil

- 1 tablespoon lemon juice

- 1 tablespoon lime juice

- 8-ounce almond milk

- ¼ cup ice cubes

Method:

1. Prepare all the ingredients and place in a blender.

2. Pulse at high speed for 1 to 2 minutes or until smooth.

3. Pour smoothie into a glass and serve.

Green Juice with Spinach

Servings: 1

Preparation time: 5 minutes

Nutrition Value:

Calories: 725 Cal, Carbs: 34.4 g, Fat: 54.7 g, Protein: 23.5 g, Fiber: 19.4 g.

Ingredients:

- 2 medium oranges, peeled

- 1 lemon, peeled

- 1 cup baby spinach

- 1 leaf of kale

- 1 scoop whey protein powder

- 2 tablespoons avocado oil

Method:

1. Prepare vegetables and fruits and rinse them thoroughly.

2. Place juicer collector under the nozzle of juicer, switch it on and process all the

   ingredients until thoroughly juiced.

3. Add protein powder into prepared juice, stir well and then stir in oil until just mixed.

4. Pour juice into a chilled glass and serve straightaway.

Green Spinach Lemonade

Servings: 1

Preparation time: 5 minutes

Nutrition Value:

Calories: 752 Cal, Carbs: 39.5 g, Fat: 56 g, Protein: 22.5 g, Fiber: 24.3 g.

Ingredients:

- 1 medium green apple, cored

- 4 leaves of kale, chopped

- 1 cup spinach, chopped

- 2 stalks of celery

- 1-inch piece of ginger

- 1 lemon

- 1 scoop whey protein powder

- 2 tablespoons avocado oil

Method:

1. Prepare vegetables and fruits and rinse them thoroughly.

2. Then cut apple and ginger into bite-size pieces.

3. Place juicer collector under the nozzle of juicer, switch it on and process all the ingredients until thoroughly juiced.

4. Pour juice in a blender, add remaining ingredients and pulse until smooth.

5. Pour juice into a chilled glass and serve straightaway.

Green Detox Juice

Servings: 1

Preparation time: 5 minutes

Nutrition Value:

Calories: 692 Cal, Carbs: 45 g, Fat: 49 g, Protein: 17.3 g, Fiber: 35.7 g.

Ingredients:

- 1 green apple, cored

- 1 cup grapes, seedless

- 1 cup pineapple, top removed

- 1 medium cucumber, peeled

- 1 lemon, peeled

- 1/2 cup parsley

- 1 scoop whey protein powder

- 2 tablespoons avocado oil

Method:

1. Prepare vegetables and fruits and rinse them thoroughly.

2. Then cut pineapple and cucumber into small pieces.

3. Place juicer collector under the nozzle of juicer, switch it on and process all the ingredients until thoroughly juiced.

4. Pour juice into a blender, add remaining ingredients and pulse until smooth.

5. Pour juice into a chilled glass and serve.

Green Ginger Ale

Servings: 1

Preparation time: 5 minutes

Nutrition Value:

Calories: 680 Cal, Carbs: 52.7 g, Fat: 49.8 g, Protein: 5.1 g, Fiber: 44.4 g.

Ingredients:

- 3 medium green apples, cored

- 1 cup spinach

- 1 medium cucumber

- 2 stalks of celery

- 1-inch piece of ginger

- 1 lime, peeled

- 2 tablespoons avocado oil

Method:

1. Prepare vegetables and fruits and rinse them thoroughly.

2. Then cut apple and cucumber into quarters.

3. Place juicer collector under the nozzle of juicer, switch it on and process all the ingredients until thoroughly juiced.

4. Add oil into prepared juice and stir well.

5. Pour juice into a chilled glass and serve straightaway.

Popeye Potion

Servings: 1

Preparation time: 5 minutes

Nutrition Value:

Calories: 604 Cal, Carbs: 43.8 g, Fat: 40.2 g, Protein: 15.1 g, Fiber: 34.4 g.

Ingredients:

- 2 medium green apples, cored

- 1/2 of a medium cucumber, peeled

- 1-inch piece of ginger

- ½ cup spinach, chopped

- ½ lemon

- 1 scoop whey protein powder

- 2 tablespoons avocado oil

Method:

1. Prepare vegetables and fruits and rinse them thoroughly.

2. Then cut apple and cucumber into quarters.

3. Place juicer collector under the nozzle of juicer, switch it on and process all the ingredients until thoroughly juiced.

4. Pour juice into a blender, add protein powder and avocado oil and pulse until smooth.

5. Pour juice into a chilled glass and serve straightaway.

Green Detox Juice

Servings: 1

Preparation time: 5 minutes

Nutrition Value:

Calories: 659 Cal, Carbs: 47.6 g, Fat: 42.3 g, Protein: 6 g, Fiber: 37.5 g.

Ingredients:

- 1 handful of spinach, chopped

- 10 sprigs of cilantro

- ½ of medium lime, peeled

- 2 medium green apples, cored

- 2 kale leaves, chopped

- 1/2 head of romaine lettuce, chopped

- 2 tablespoons avocado oil

Method:

1. Prepare vegetables and fruits and rinse them thoroughly.

2. Then cut apples into quarters and chop spinach and kale.

3. Place juicer collector under the nozzle of juicer, switch it on and process all the ingredients until thoroughly juiced.

4. Add oil into prepared juice and stir well.

5. Pour juice into a chilled glass and serve straightaway.

Deep Green Juice

Servings: 1

Preparation time: 5 minutes

Nutrition Value:

Calories: 577 Cal, Carbs: 43.2 g, Fat: 41 g, Protein: 8.6 g, Fiber: 23.6 g.

Ingredients:

- 1 green apple, peeled and cored

- 6 leaves of collard

- 1 medium cucumber, peeled

- 2 celery ribs

- 1/2 of lemon, peeled

- 2 tablespoons avocado oil

Method:

1. Prepare vegetables and fruits and rinse them thoroughly.

2. Then cut the apple into quarters.

3. Place juicer collector under the nozzle of juicer, switch it on and process all the

   ingredients until thoroughly juiced.

4. Add oil into prepared juice and stir well.

5. Pour juice into a chilled glass and serve straightaway.

Kale and Kiwi Green Juice

Servings: 1

Preparation time: 5 minutes

Nutrition Value:

Calories: 690 Cal, Carbs: 58.6 g, Fat: 48.3 g, Protein: 5.1 g, Fiber: 43.8 g.

Ingredients:

- 2 green apples, peeled and cored

- 3 kiwi fruits

- 1 bunch of kale leaves

- 1-inch piece of ginger

- 2 tablespoons avocado oil

Method:

1. Prepare vegetables and fruits and rinse them thoroughly.

2. Then cut apple and kiwi into quarters.

3. Place juicer collector under the nozzle of juicer, switch it on and process all the ingredients until thoroughly juiced.

4. Add oil into prepared juice and stir well.